US COLLEGE GUIDE

SECURING YOUR DREAM US COLLEGE OFFERS

JOSHUA J. W. YEN

Copyright Joshua J.W. Yen 2023 All legal and moral rights reserved.

No part of this book may be reproduced, distributed, or transmitted in any form or by any electronic or mechanical means without the prior written permission of the publisher, except in the case of quotations embodied in reviews of this book or as permitted by copyright law.

By way of non-exhaustive example this means that you must not photocopy, record, extract, adapt, translate or convert any part to other media forms.

Author: Joshua J. W. Yen joshuajwyen@gmail.com

Cover and interior design: Andy Meaden www.meadencreative.com

Publisher: Barry J. Yen barry64@gmail.com

The domain names www.josh-yen.com, www.joshuajwyen.com and www.logos-education.com, as well as all content, belong to Joshua J. W. Yen

Joshua also provides university application advice on his website www.logos-education.com and on the Logos Education YouTube channel https://bit.ly/logosyt

CONTENTS

Introduction	1
How to make the most of this book	1
Who this book is for	6
Get Your Life in Order	13
Where you are now	15
Your identity and vision	18
How much time do you have?	23
The University Admission time-frame	23
What does University mean to you?	29
Mastering US Application Fundamentals	39
Boring Admin Stuff	41
Building healthy relationships with teachers	48
What are Admission Officers looking for?	52
Determining which universities you submit to	55
The One-Application-Dream-Offers Method	71
1. Preparing your application	73
2. Writing your application	82
3. Writing your Personal Essay	83
4. Writing your Activities and Honours List	91
5. Writing your Supplemental Essay	93
Editing Your Application	99
Conclusion	105
About the Author	113

INTRODUCTION

HOW TO MAKE THE MOST OF THIS BOOK

This book was written with three goals in mind:

Goal 1: To guide you through the US Application process.
Goal 2: To provide you with the information you need to get into your dream universities.
Goal 3: To direct you to additional tools which may help you along the way.

By accomplishing these goals, I believe the book would put you (or your child) in a very good position to get offers from your dream universities. It doesn't matter what stage of your high school career you are at now, be it Grade 8 or your Senior year. If you follow the advice given in this book, I believe you will have a better understanding of what you need to do to succeed in the hyper-competitive field of university applications.

In order to achieve this goal, I will be sharing with you the **One-Application-Dream-Offers Method**—a method

I developed by analysing successful applications to some of the best US universities, like Harvard, Columbia, the University of Chicago, UCLA, and more. What is special about this method is not just that it can get you into your dream universities: it does so by helping you to remain authentic — to stay strong to your ideals without having to do or say anything just for the sake of getting into a university.

I'm going to be transparent about how this book will work. If you are looking for something to reinforce your preconceived ideas about the university application process, you may as well throw the book away. But if you want the cold, harsh truth about where you are at, what you need to do, and how you can do it, then read on, and pay attention!

HELP ME TO HELP YOU!

I'm going to write this book in a conversational and direct tone. I am not here to reinforce your misconceptions about university admissions, I will give you the facts bluntly and directly to help you create an application which will help you get into your dream universities. As such, I have structured the book as follows:

First, I will address you, the student, as an individual, telling you how you can put yourself in the best position to prepare your application and get into your dream universities.

Secondly, I will take you through the fundamentals of the US application system: the forms you have to fill in, what admission officers are looking for, and (perhaps more exciting) how you should choose which universities to apply to.

Finally, I will introduce you to the **One-Application-Dream-Offers Method**. This will tell you how you can prepare, write, and edit your essays, supplemental essays and activity lists to make sure that, regardless of your starting point, you will be able to submit a competitive university application.

By the time you finish reading this book, I hope you will be motivated to start working on your US applications, and (more importantly) that you will be filled with self-belief that you *can* get into your dream universities. Of course, I can only put so much information into one book. That is why I will be directing you to additional materials to turn to for further guidance and advice.

BE CONFIDENT! DON'T UNDERESTIMATE YOUR POTENTIAL!

You may be feeling overwhelmed. This is a natural reaction! Whatever you do now will impact what you will be doing over the next 4+ years of your life! Therefore it is important to make sure that everything is done purposefully and with your goals in mind.

I like to compare life to a game of chess. What you do impacts on not just the next few moves, but also can have a 'butterfly' effect on what happens further down the line — if not right to the endgame itself. Therefore, it is important that you think everything through before you decide to commit to anything, and be perspicacious enough to avoid making needless mistakes in your life.

There is a common misconception that, when it comes to university applications, the process is an insuperable labyrinth that only a few people can unlock. The reality is that searching for this 'one way' or this 'one strategy' will never work. The more you try it, the more time you are wasting, and you are setting yourself up for failure.

Anyone at a top university will tell you that all the people they have met there have different backgrounds, stories, and ways to present their application. This is not a dig at those people who claim to have a single set of things you need to do for success: it may have worked for them. Rather, it is unrealistic to expect that the same method would necessarily work for you.

It is for this reason that the **One-Application-Dream-Offers Method** does not offer a set program that you must follow. Rather, the **One-Application-Dream-Offers Method** promotes a way of life which anyone can adopt and implement, which, over time and with discipline, will mould you into the ideal candidate—the ideal human being—to overcome any challenges that you will face in the future.

So, my message to you right now is that you should not be afraid of the perceived complexity of university applications. Put some trust in yourself. Reading this book will put you on the right track and direct you to any additional tools, should you ever need that extra help! As long as you are willing to be humble and take on board the lessons found here, you will be one step closer to achieving those dream offers!

I would like to end this chapter by congratulating you for taking your Common App seriously, for recognizing that there are things you might not know which could increase your chances of getting into your dream universities. Humility and openness to new knowledge is vital for success in every field of human endeavour. The most successful people I know constantly reflect on themselves, strive for self-improvement, demand more from themselves, and (most importantly), when faced with something that they do not know, are willing to look for the help that they need in order to succeed. Of course, university admissions are a very competitive field, and it is impossible to guarantee success; but what I can say is that by following the **One-Application-Dream-Offers Method**, you will stand out amongst the rest!

Message from Josh:
Be purposeful in everything you do! Understand why you are doing it, and why you need to do it!

WHO THIS BOOK IS FOR

In the world we live in today, we like instant gratification. In the past, people had to walk to the nearest library to borrow a book to search for information: now we can just go onto our phones. In the past people had to travel to the nearest city to buy groceries: now we can order them to our doorstep.

If you have bought this book thinking that the **One-Application-Dream-Offers Method** is going to help you get into your dream university without your needing to put in effort — I'm sorry to disappoint you: that won't work!

I have always stressed that the true spirit of university admissions is encapsulated in hard work, determination, and commitment which goes beyond doing the bare minimum. It is the constant pursuit of self-improvement which will get you in the right place, and allow you to build a phenomenal portfolio to face the multitude of challenges in life. It is a path which, although difficult, will help anyone, *regardless* of their background, get into their dream universities.

> *Note from Josh*
> *If you make your last two years of High School only about getting into universities, you will feel miserable if that fails. However, if you focus on yourself, you will come out of this process having bettered yourself and put yourself in a better place to overcome any obstacle regardless of your university offers.*

You might think I am crazy for making the bold statement that anyone can get themselves into their dream university. Let me illustrate!

During my last two years in High School, I spent quite a lot of time analysing different students and their respective university offers. It was during the start of Senior year that two truths became blatantly obvious:

Truth 1: People normally got what they deserved.
Truth 2: Natural-born talent rarely influenced their success as an applicant.

Let me illustrate these truths with a few different categories of students that we, as fellow students, are familiar with.

CATEGORY 1: LITTLE TALENT, LOW MOTIVATION

This is neither the smartest nor the most motivated kid in the classroom. He tries his best to get by school while doing the smallest amount of work possible. He's the kid who doesn't show up to class most of the time due to an inexplicable illness; and when he is not sick, he is looking to copy last week's homework off his mates. Now this lack of motivation may not be due to any inherent flaw on his part. He probably looked around the classroom, saw everyone doing way better than him, and immediately thought "Nope, I'm out, I'm not going to compete with these people".

This isn't meant as an insult towards this student. In my experience, these are some of the nicest people you would meet. Firstly, they have to maintain good relationships with people to copy their homework! But jokes aside, they normally like the simple things in life: they play football at break, watch anime, and play video games. When it comes to uni offers, in line with their general attitude, they often submit a half-hearted application and fail to achieve their full potential. That being said, they are probably not too irritated by the results, as their mindset tells them that they weren't meant to do as well as everyone else, and they will perhaps not be too affected.

CATEGORY 2: LITTLE TALENT, HIGH MOTIVATION

The second category is a bit different to the first. They similarly lack talent, but they have this inner drive which makes them put in double the work that everyone else does. They look around at the more talented students and are determined that, with hard work, they will be able to keep up with, if not out-perform, those around them.

You may not see them at the club, or at the heart of social circles, but you also know that they are at home working hard, making the most of every opportunity to get a head-start over their competition.

When it comes to university applications, these students take them very seriously, and they often put a lot of effort into making sure that their application is in the right place to get them into their dream universities. In my experience, these students normally do very well in their applications, oftentimes even out-performing those in the 'high talent, low motivation' category.

CATEGORY 3: AVERAGE TALENT, AVERAGE MOTIVATION

Then you have the group of kids who perform quite averagely in school. They don't need to put in too much effort to get where they want to be academically, and do just enough to get respectable grades in High School. Like the students in

Category 1, they most likely do not expect too much from themselves, and are definitely less demanding of themselves than those in Category 2.

In Year 13, they probably spend a few weeks putting together a good application before sending it off to their universities. Since their portfolios are most likely a mix of activities they have worked on over the years, it is probably not too bad; though it may not be the best way to get into their dream universities. Therefore, while they may not end up with the best offers, they most likely would enter a reputable institution and be happy with it.

CATEGORY 4: HIGH TALENT, LOW MOTIVATION

Let's face it, we all know them, and find this group of people somewhat irritating. These are the kids who game or party the night before the test, but, as usual, they end up with some of the highest scores in the class, and end up celebrating with even more booze. They grow up surrounded by A* or 4.0 grades and have been taught to believe that everything in academics will be a breeze.

Therefore, they often view their applications as something that can be completed half-heartedly yet still be successful. They're not completely wrong. In my experience, some of them do get into highly-respectable universities, but the majority of them end up in the same universities as the 'average talent, average motivation' category.

In the end, they are probably a bit disappointed with the fact that people with low talent out-perform them: but they don't really care too much about it, because they still are at a respectable university, and can perhaps party even more there.

CATEGORY 5: HIGH TALENT, HIGH MOTIVATION

These students exemplify the height of what can be achieved in High School. They are quite an elusive group of students in school. Like the low talent, high motivation kids, they are rarely seen at the club, or out and about socially. They are often either studying, or working on some mad project to save the world—or they have a lofty goal that they are working towards which the rest of us can barely wrap our heads around. As expected, these students are those who receive the best university offers: these are the students going to Harvard, Princeton, or Columbia, amongst other top universities.

Of course, this list of student types isn't exclusive, and everyone falls somewhere on an axis of talent and motivation. However, this image will help you develop your understanding of what makes a good applicant, and that the differentiating factor is not just about talent, but about one's motivation and effort. By going the extra mile, we can see that the low talent student is able to out-compete his peers, and to compete with the results of the high-talented and highly-motivated student in admissions.

This is something I love about US admissions. By emphasising the need for a holistic student, one is less defined by a single metric (like academics); and a student who is perspicacious enough to recognize his weaknesses can level the playing field by making sure that the rest of their application is very strong.

This is why I wrote this book and developed the **One-Application-Dream-Offers Method**, to demonstrate to you and convince you that anyone, regardless of their starting point, can put together a good application and get into their dream universities.

So, if you entered into university admissions thinking that the people around you are way too talented to compete with, think again! It doesn't matter which category you fall into; it doesn't matter if you weren't born with talent. You can do it! Make sure that you focus on improving yourself every day, and be aware of everything you are doing!

If you are willing to dream bigger, to push yourself to your limit, to face problems with determination, then I am confident that, regardless of your starting point, you will do well.

In the end, the most important thing is that you can look at yourself in the mirror every day and be proud of yourself. In the long term, your university doesn't matter too much. Yes, it will give you a significant head-start; but most of the people I admire in the world did not go to a university that I have ever heard of. However, if you are happy with yourself, you are confident, and you do the best in everything you do, you will go far in the applications process, and beyond.

GET YOUR LIFE IN ORDER

"Set your house in perfect order before you criticise the world."

Jordan Peterson, *12 Rules for Life: an Antidote to Chaos*

There are two reasons why this quote is greatly applicable to any applicant aiming for their dream universities:

Reason 1: This book is meant to throw you out of your comfort zone.
Reason 2: This quote is at the core of the **One-Application-Dream-Offers Method** mentality.

Let me elaborate.

Building upon my message in the introduction, I do not aim to tell you what you want to hear: rather I'm going to tell you what you *need* to hear. Similar to most things in life, if you are continuously doing something wrong, it is most likely that you are very comfortable with whatever you are doing incorrectly. Sometimes, when you are in such a place in life, all you need is a strong kick up the backside to make sure you get back on track. For example, in High School, you might be easing your way through your math course without putting in too much effort, until a new topic comes up and you get 30% on a test, reminding you that the subject deserves more attention than you thought.

That is the purpose of this book. I want to wake you up from your slumber so that you can drive yourself to success. That being said, I do know people whose lives are already set in order: if this is the case—good for you! This book will give you the final things that you can tweak in order to achieve success.

I believe that the above quote is the epitome of the **One-Application-Dream-Offers Method**. I don't mean that university admissions are a form of criticising the world, or that tidying up your house would increase your chances of getting into your dream university. I believe however that the essence of Dr. Peterson's message is highly applicable. When planning your university admissions journey, you may be tempted to make an artificial checklist in your mind of things you must do in order to get into your dream universities. However, that would be similar to what Dr. Peterson calls "criticising the world". Instead of starting with an intrinsic change, it focuses on *things* to change which may or may not represent who you really are.

The **One-Application-Dream-Offers Method** teaches you to start first with your individual self, which will then be demonstrated by your acts. Therefore: get yourself, your story, and your identity in order before you start your university admissions process, and (trust me) it will make it way easier for you in more aspects than you could possibly realise.

Think about it from the Admissions Officers' perspective: would they prefer a genuine student with good mentality and values, or a **fraud** who attempts to **fake** his way to success? In fact, put that aside: could you truly look yourself in the mirror and accept that you are a **fraud** lying your way to whatever you perceive to be success? I hope the answer is NO.

The reality is that I know a lot of people who have tried to cheat the system; and while I won't name what they have done, you can rest assured that the best universities they got into were my 'safeties' (explained further down!). At the end of the day, it always boils down to this one message:

HAVE INTEGRITY! EVERYTHING ELSE WILL FOLLOW!

WHERE YOU ARE NOW

"Know yourself and know your enemy. You will win every battle."

Sun Tzu, The Art of War

In order to get to where you want to be, it is important first to understand who you are, and who you are up against. By doing this you will be able to take advantage of every single weakness that your competition may have, and make it more difficult for your competition to do the same to you!

A quick disclaimer: while it is good to recognize that a lot of your peers will be competing for your spots, don't view them as your enemies. They are your friends, and that is more important. In fact, I would go so far as to say that having a tight group of friends actively working towards helping each other get into their dream universities would actually be a net positive for everyone involved, even if you are applying to *exactly the same* universities.

That said, you should remember that university admissions are very personal, and do have a big impact on one's life. Therefore, I would recommend that you approach this topic with great care whenever it is brought up, especially with close friends.

Know thy competition
Let us start off by discussing Sun Tzu's maxim of "knowing thy enemy", which I believe would help you to understand

your competition, and also to know how you could analyse your own weaknesses.

In order to understand your competition, it is important that you start paying attention to the sample group before you—your year-group (and perhaps the year above, for a larger pool). By understanding what the average student is doing, you will begin to notice different things which you can take advantage of. Are some of them addicted to video games? Are some of them partying three nights a week? These are all things you can take advantage of in order to out-compete your opposition.

Now, I am not promoting complete withdrawal from society, the progression of the youth to a monastery! It's all right to play a weekly game of *Fortnight*, it's all right to go clubbing occasionally. Just make sure you are aware of what people are doing to compete for your spot, and that it doesn't put you at a disadvantage.

After all, universities are structured into a pyramid with an upper limit. If you can achieve a certain section of the pyramid, let's say the top 50 universities, in the Common App while enjoying a party once a month, go ahead! If you can do that while partying more, go ahead! Just make sure you won't regret it if you end up missing your goal in the end.

> **Reminder from Josh**
> *While uni applications are important, the process is not the be-all and end-all of High School. You are only going to have these precious years once. So make sure you are enjoying yourself. I was lucky to have football on the side: maybe you have another sport or hobby which you can use to connect with your friends. Don't throw it away in the chase for university goals! It would never be worth it!*

YOUR IDENTITY AND VISION

KNOW THYSELF

Now that we have talked about how you can know more about your competition, I would like to spend some time discussing how you can learn more about yourself. I would like to approach this from two perspectives. Firstly, to help you find out your weaknesses; secondly, to help you understand the time-frame of university applications.

REALITY-CHECK EXERCISE

Before we get started, I would like you to fill out this exercise to help you get a good idea of how prepared you are for getting into your dream universities. For each statement, give yourself a rating of 1 to 10 in terms of accuracy. Remember, you are the only person who is going to read this, so you should try to be as honest as possible to make the most out of it!

Readiness Statement	Self-rating (1-10)
I feel like I make good use of my time.	
I feel like I have good self-control.	
I feel like my academics are going very well.	
I feel like my extracurricular life is composed of various pursuits, academic, sports, musical, etc.	
I consistently achieve the goals I set myself.	
I have a long time left in High School.	
I feel that I am achieving my full potential right now.	
I know exactly what I need to do to get into the top universities.	
I know what I want to study in university.	
I know what my future career plan is (not what you actually will be doing, but what you think or want to be doing).	
Total	

After you have completed this table, you can check your total score against the following answer-key to see where you are at. Of course, this isn't a perfect test, but it will give you a good understanding of where you are in the application journey.

0-60: A LONG WAY TO GO

If you fall into this category, it means that you still have a lot to do in order to get yourself prepared for university applications. Don't worry! When I first started thinking about university applications in my Junior year, I fell into this category. However, with the **One-Application-Dream-Offers Method**, I was still able to get into some of the best universities, so do not be disheartened.

There are probably three reasons why you have fallen into this category. Firstly, you still have many years ahead of you and the idea of university has just come into your mind. There's nothing wrong with this. If you are in Grade 7 or Grade 8, getting into university shouldn't be the first thing you care about! Secondly, you might not have taken your academics seriously, and while you may have a decent set of extracurriculars, you are very far from where you want to be academically. If that's the case, you might need to work harder! Finally, you may be in your Senior year, with university admissions right around the corner, and you really do not know what to do! Buying this book was a last-ditch 'Hail Mary', hopefully to get your application in order.

Regardless of which of these apply to you, understand that you still can get into your dream university! Just make sure to take on board all of the advice.

60-80: GETTING CLOSER

If you fall into this category, then it shows that you have been getting along quite well with your university applications. Even if you haven't started thinking about them in too much depth, you have been working hard and have made sure that you have not slacked off with your studies. By doing this, you would have naturally placed yourself in a very good position for university admissions.

That being said, you may still have some uncertainties about what you want to do in the future, and do not know what the best way is to spend your time and effort in preparing for your applications. You should read this book to get a better understanding of the university application process, and give yourself a clear direction and plan for how you will get from where you are now to your dream universities.

80+: NEARLY THERE

Congratulations. Very few people can get into this category unless they have a very well-organised life and have done some preparation for their university admissions.

This book will help you get the final pieces of the puzzle in place, give you a new perspective into university admissions, and ultimately help you get into your dream universities.

FINDING YOUR WEAKNESSES

In the section above, we discussed how you can find the weaknesses of your competition. However, these are only the actions which you can observe. I am a strong believer that the most important aspects of life are your intrinsic attributes — those which cannot be observed. These are attributes like hard work, integrity, determination, and more.

While university applications boils down to showing people what you can do, your applications will become so much stronger when they come from the right place. If you are working for a charity only for a university offer, what would happen if it came up in an interview? It is very easy for a seasoned interviewer to tell whether you are being genuine or not! Even if you don't require an interview, a seasoned Admissions Officer can tell from your application whether certain activities fit into your overall story, or whether they are totally out of place. The **One-Application-Dream-Offers Method** values the development of a good individual above everything else.

Therefore, make sure that everything you do is working towards developing your identity and values. This will take you far, both in university admissions and beyond. If you find any weaknesses in your mental strength, your intrinsic skills, or your personality, High School is the opportune time to work on these weaknesses and develop yourself further, as you don't have much to lose and everything to gain.

HOW MUCH TIME DO YOU HAVE?

THE UNIVERSITY ADMISSION TIME-FRAME

Since this book is written for all students thinking about US admissions, I recognize that there will be a great diversity among the readers. While most of you are probably Juniors, approaching the last two years of High School, I recognize that a lot of people may start their university admissions preparation from a younger age—Grade 8 or below. Therefore, I have separated this next section into different sections, depending on how old you are right now!

GRADE 8 OR YOUNGER

If you are currently a Grade 8 student: good news! you have a long way ahead. For the moment, I would recommend that you not think too much about university admissions. While you can do things to help your application, you have many years to think about this, and should have more pressing priorities on your mind.

Use this time to diversify your interests. Try new sports, musical instruments, different activities, and also read a lot of books. Go on Google, and do a simple search for the best five books on a certain topic. Read two of these books, then choose a different subject and read a few on that. If you like a particular topic, then focus on it a bit more: maybe read the other three books.

This will prepare you for the future. With university admissions, you would be able to demonstrate a breadth of knowledge, allowing you to make an informed choice when it comes to choosing a course for university. With life, you would be able to talk to almost anyone you meet. When meeting people in my travels, I have been very grateful for my knowledge about sports, different academic fields, music, and more, holding conversations with fascinating people and building connections with them.

FRESHMAN YEAR

If you are in Freshman year, make sure that you have chosen the right subjects for your upcoming exams; this could be your GCSEs or your APs (depending on which education system you follow). Not only will this dictate what options you have in the future; it will also help you to focus on the disciplines that you will be interested in studying.

While you should still be searching for what you are interested in, this is a time to add depth to your activities. If you have been trying loads of different sports, you could pick one or two which you enjoy, and get very good at it. The same theory applies to other activities as well. Of course, you still have a lot of time to try out new things; but in order to be competitive, you need to show the Admission Officers that not only can you do a lot of things, but that you can also do some of them very well.

SOPHOMORE YEAR

If you are in Sophomore year, you should make sure that any choice of subjects for your exams (A Levels, IB or AP) would keep the doors open for potential changes to your future plans. If you are thinking that you might want to do a course that has pre-requisite requirements for a certain subject, or that knowledge in a certain subject would demonstrate interest in that course, then that may be something you should choose.

On the extracurricular front, you could draw a mind-map of your activities and how they tie into your different interests, expertise, or 'selling-points'. You will notice that a lot of your skills are linked together, and support different strengths. If you notice that some activities are unrelated to your 'selling points', then you should consider whether those are the right things to carry on with in the long term. Remember, everything you do should be deliberate; so if something isn't positively helping you to develop, both for university and for life, you might want to consider cutting it out.

> *Advice from Josh*
> *You shouldn't get rid of **everything** which doesn't help you accomplish your goals. It probably isn't best for your mental health if the only thing you do is **study**. Apart from my academics and extracurriculars, I used to spend time playing **Rise of Kingdoms**, **CS:GO**, and **Football Manager**, which helped me manage my academic stress and pressure.*

JUNIOR YEAR

If you are in Junior Year, you don't have that much time left. In previous years, you had more time to experiment with different things, but with the start of your A-Levels or IB, you have more responsibilities and exams.

You should also spend more time thinking about what you want to study in university, and what your career plans are. It would become more and more difficult to maintain all of your extracurricular activities, so make sure that you become more focused. Of course, if you have only just started your university admissions process, and have not actually done enough extracurricular activities, it might be more difficult for you to build a successful CV. However, by being focused on a handful of pursuits, you will be able to make up for lost time and build a successful application.

SENIOR YEAR

If you are reading this book at the start of your Senior Year, not having thought much about university admissions, you have a lot ahead of you to do. This is not to say that all hope is lost: far from it! The first thing you need to do is to make sure that you do very well in the first exams of the year, to boost your grades and your academic profile.

Then, make sure that you immediately make a mind-map of what extracurricular activities you have done so far. As long as you haven't spent all your time gaming and clubbing, you should have used a lot of your High School years working on some extracurricular activities which would be beneficial for your applications. By identifying what these are, you will be able to develop them further to help boost your CV.

However, if you really haven't done anything at all, what you need to do is choose the course you would apply to, and read the top 10 books in the discipline. Building an academic portfolio is way more time-efficient than getting good at an extracurricular activity. By reading ten books (a 200-page book normally takes me two days to finish), you would probably know more about a certain discipline than most of the students who are applying to your course! On the other hand, it is probably hard enough to get into your school's varsity team or orchestra as a seasoned athlete or musician, let alone as someone who picks up sport or music for the first time. Therefore, by maximizing what you can change, you would be able to build a more convincing academic profile.

> ***Lesson from Josh***
> *Most of my friends who have gotten into the very top US universities have academic profiles. While there is an impression that extracurricular activities are the be-all and end-all of US applications, there is no reason to believe that being academically-focused would put you at a disadvantage.*

In this section, you might have realized that I didn't talk about getting good grades. This is not because getting good grades isn't important. In fact, it is the complete opposite. Everyone who applies to the top universities already has good grades. Never give yourself an excuse to not be ahead and in control of your academic work. Of course, good grades will always be subject to your experience and your background. However, what is objective is your effort.

To conclude: if you are still in Grade 8, relax! You still have a lot of time: just make sure you are doing the basics right. Experiment with new things—you have a long time to figure out what you truly want. However, if you are in your Senior Year, maybe it's time to up the stakes a bit more and focus on maximising your efforts with the short time that you have. I recognize that this is a difficult process, and that you might feel overwhelmed with how you are meant to plan the next years of your High School. Don't worry, that is completely natural. If you would like to reach out and book a 1-1 session with me, you can do that on my website at https://www.logos-education.com/consulting.

WHAT DOES UNIVERSITY MEAN TO YOU?

In university applications, it is very easy to think about what other people want from you. This could be your parents, your teachers, or your significant other. While you should take their advice into consideration, it is easy to forget the most important part of the journey—what you want!

As much as we want to tell ourselves that what we do right now doesn't matter too much: a case can be made that your university admissions journey embodies the most influential decision you have faced so far. What university you go to will dictate what you will be doing for the next few years of your life. It will determine the type of people you will meet, what facilities and activities you will have access to, and will have an influence over some of the job opportunities that you have in the future. Of course, success in life is not just determined by the university you go to, but by how you make the most of individual opportunities as they arise. However, the university does help to boost your initial 'reputation' and 'status', giving you a head-start over the rest.

Why do I place such emphasis on university admissions?

In reality, it isn't the university admissions process that I am focusing on. Rather, I am placing an emphasis on the impact that the process can have on your life. Even if your teachers and your parents want the best for you, you need to recognise that it is ultimately your life that is being impacted. You need to prioritise yourself, and what you want! But in order to do that, you must know what you want to do, and where you want to be! Therefore, I will spend some time exploring this topic.

To get started, I am not talking about a set plan or dream that you will follow till you die. Dreams change, aspirations change. As you meet new people, are exposed to new information, and experience new possibilities, it is natural for your goals and dreams to change. For example, if you asked a Grade-8 Josh what he wanted to do in the future, compared to the Senior-Year Josh, compared to the uni Josh, you would probably be given significantly different answers.

Having said this, you may be curious as to how anyone can decide anything about their university goals. That is a justified concern. In fact, most of the people I know who have applied, or are applying to universities, have little or no clue as to what they will do after university.

This is what I like about the US system. During your US applications, while you can specify a major, you are only temporarily committing yourself to that major: it isn't something that you must follow until the day you graduate. This allows for you to specify a specific discipline when applying to university, but also to make changes later if you realize that you would be better off doing something else. As a result, just think about what you want to do now, and if this changes in the future, you should have the opportunity to change it when the time comes.

So what are some ways to help you figure out what you want?

The first thing that you should think about are your fundamental priorities in life. By understanding your fundamental priorities, you will have a better understanding of what you might want to achieve. Let me use myself as an example.

My priorities in order of importance are as follows:

Priority 1: Serve God.
Priority 2: Family.
Priority 3: Achieve financial freedom.
Priority 4: Serve the wider community.
Priority 5: Make a name for myself.

You will notice that these priorities are not reliant on external circumstances, and could be applied to every situation that I am thrown into. Of course, at times I might focus more on my business, Logos Education, a college counselling and mentoring service; at others I might spend more time focusing on academics. But these are only secondary goals, which are influenced by my five main priorities in life. In the same way, if you discover your priorities, you will have a better picture of how you want to progress, and what you want to get from university.

DISCOVER YOUR PRIORITIES EXERCISE

While I don't expect you to have critically analyzed your priorities before, I would like you to try to fill out some of your fundamental and secondary priorities in order of importance. Spend some time thinking about what things mean most to you, and how they have been applied to your decision-making in the past.

While I will give you five spaces for the fundamental priority list, and ten spaces for the secondary priority list, do not feel pressure to fill them all out, or to reduce them to those numbers. Just fill out what you think, and it will be a very helpful way in getting to understand more about yourself!

FUNDAMENTAL PRIORITIES

1. _____
2. _____
3. _____
4. _____
5. _____

SECONDARY PRIORITIES

1. _____
2. _____
3. _____
4. _____
5. _____
6. _____

7. _____
8. _____
9. _____
10. _____

Now that you have filled out this list, I would like you to think back about how these priorities might tie into your university applications process. How would a specific course or university help you achieve these priorities?

For example, studying philosophy and theology at Oxford is probably quite a good decision for some of my priorities. I am at one of the most historic universities in the world, with a beautiful cathedral and a phenomenal Christian community (helping my first priority); then, philosophy and theology struggle with questions of existential significance, furthering my understanding of mankind as a whole (helping my first and fourth priority); and I am given the opportunity of putting a phenomenal university on my CV, and of meeting interesting and successful people (helping my second and fifth goals indirectly). Of course, it isn't a perfect match: philosophy and theology probably aren't a perfect or direct match for financial freedom, so that is why I do quite a lot of other things on the side as well. However, this example gives you a good framework for understanding how your university might fit into your different life-goals. In fact, it was for these reasons that I decided to turn down Columbia and go to Oxford instead. Likewise, when my good friend Warren chose Harvard over Cambridge, going to Harvard suited his priorities better than Cambridge did.

Now that we have talked a bit about how better to understand what your university decisions mean to you, I would like to spend some time discussing how you can understand what course you would like to pursue. While this is less important than if studying in the UK, understanding approximately what disciplines you are interested in can help you structure and develop your application.

To help you choose your preferred course, I would like to return to a suggestion I raised earlier: to read many different books about different topics and disciplines until you settle on something you are really interested in. By doing so, you would not only be able to use that information to back up your arguments, but you would also be able to discover what you want to study academically. I also recommend that you listen to lectures on YouTube, or to podcasts, about different topics. If a particular course provides you with loads of insight and greatly interests you, it might also be a good indicator that you should apply to that course.

> *Tip from Josh*
> *A lot of big universities like Yale or Harvard upload lecture-series to YouTube. These would not only allow you to learn about the different teaching styles; they would also indicate to you whether you truly wanted to study that particular course. They would also give you extra material to discuss in your application, especially in the supplemental essays.*

While there is an option to apply as "undecided" (that is without a major in mind), I would not recommend that you do this. Firstly, how are you meant to demonstrate your academic pursuits apart from your grades? It would seem ridiculous to write your essays on every discipline known to mankind: but if you only wrote your essays on philosophy (as an example), then one would question why you didn't just apply to study philosophy as your major.

Therefore, while it isn't impossible to provide a good academic profile while applying as "undecided", I believe that declaring a major would be a good way to structure your application, and make sure that you have an application which remains consistent and to the point.

After understanding what university means to you, and how you can decide your major, I would like to end this chapter with a controversial question:

SHOULD YOU GO TO UNIVERSITY?

Imagine: you are in your Senior year right now: you are reading this book, and no matter how hard you want to fit a course or a university into your priorities, none of them seem to fit you! You might be wanting to become an entrepreneur, pursue a sporting career, or embark on a type of trade. In this circumstance, you may be asking yourself whether it would be still worth going to university.

I would like to make the argument that in 90% of circumstances, going to university, or at least submitting an application, would be worth it (assuming that finances are not an issue). After all, university isn't all about the course, but also about the people you will meet, the connections you will build, and the soft skills that you will acquire along the way. Even if you aren't thinking about pursuing the course as part of your future profession, it is still a wonderful time of your life, and an important symbolic stage into maturity. You will live on your own, perhaps in a different country; you will meet new people, and be exposed to new beliefs, ideas, and customs. You will have to fend for yourself, and will have to take on a new set of responsibilities. However, it also means that you will be able to get used to a new freedom, and be exposed to a form of carefreeness in the world. As such, university would most likely be a good choice for you.

That being said, I do believe there may be a few situations where university might not be for you. If you are an extremely talented sports-person on the verge of signing a professional or semi-professional contract, then pursuing your dreams might be a reasonable thing to do. Likewise with music, or another trade—your ambitions might be so great that an entire course at university would do nothing but hinder your chance at achieving your goal. You need to recognize that university is a huge time-commitment, and that it will take up most of your time during the week. Therefore, just as I want you to be perspicacious in maximizing your efforts in getting into your dream university, you should use a similar mindset to judge whether university fits into your broader plans.

I am not telling you not to apply. I am sure most of your parents would definitely not be very happy with me for even raising this as an option! However, I recognize that there are people who want to achieve goals in which university isn't a reasonable choice. I also recognize that in order to accomplish certain things, you have to take risks and make sacrifices to have the chance of achieving them. So—this is something I just want to place on the table.

For most people reading this, the possibility shouldn't even be on the table. However, for a select few (and I think you probably already know who you are), this is something that you should potentially consider. After all, it goes back to my fundamental message to you:

THIS IS YOUR LIFE! YOU MAKE THE DECISIONS, YOU TAKE RESPONSIBILITY!

I hope this chapter has helped you understand more about yourself and how your university admissions can fit into your vision for the future. I completely understand that this is a very big decision! It was less than three years ago that I was wrestling with the same challenges that you are facing.

So, if you feel a bit overwhelmed, or that you want to stop and think a bit more about your direction in life, take all the time you need! Slow down, put the book down, maybe go for a jog or walk round the block. Think slowly about your vision and your identity. Once you get that sorted, you will be unstoppable!

MASTERING US APPLICATION FUNDAMENTALS

"The rain came down, the streams rose, and the winds blew and beat against that house [built on sand], and it fell with a great crash."

Matthew 7:24 (NIV)

When you suddenly get a burst of motivation, or a 'eureka!' moment in getting something accomplished, it is very easy to throw yourself at the project before you have gotten the fundamentals sorted. You feel proud to have gotten everything set up and ready for submission: then, upon closer analysis, you realize that half of the admin stuff is missing — and your application is all over the place, without any sense of direction.

This may seem like an exaggeration, but it's a very easy trap to fall into when you are starting out on your university applications. With so much emphasis put on your essays and activities list, it is easy to finish the 'more important', and honestly more interesting, part of the application without thinking about what a good application is, and what the other things are that you need to submit.

Therefore, I would like to spend some time talking about the fundamentals of the university applications process. These include, of course, the very boring admin stuff; how you can improve your grades and referral letters; and also more exciting things—like what university Admissions Officers are looking for. By understanding these fundamentals, it will guide you through the rest of the application, giving you a clear mental framework which you should base the idea around.

If you have read the accompanying book on UK admissions, you will have found the material up until now to be relatively similar. The reason for this is that since I recognize that many people may apply to universities in both the US and the UK (something that I recommend you do), it is better to kill two birds with one stone than to live two separate lives in preparing for your applications. However, from now on, you will find that the material will become different, in order to accommodate for the differences between the two systems and give you the best chances to get into your dream universities.

Furthermore, since this book is written to cover how to apply on all the application platforms in the US—like the Common App, UCs, and more—I would like to make it clear that not everything in this section is applicable to each individual application platform. For example, there is only one personal essay for the Common App, whereas the UCs request you to write four essays, to be sent to all the universities. Nevertheless, I do believe that the overall requirements, of having to submit grades, essays, and an activity list, are universally applicable. Therefore, this book will cover all of these topics together.

BORING ADMIN STUFF

Let's face it, no one likes admin requirements and filling out forms. However, it is highly advisable to get this out of the way the moment you start your application process. You want to spend most of your time thinking about things which would actually make a difference in your admissions—for example, your essays, supplemental essays, and activity lists. Therefore, I intend to zoom through this chapter as quickly as possible, give brief tips and advice on how to optimize this process, and then carry on to the more important stuff.

A quick note before getting started. Since this book covers all the application platforms in the US system, it is impossible for me to cover each in depth. Therefore, while the advice and tips can be applied to all, make sure you double-check with the website to make sure that you are up to date with the latest information.

DEADLINES

Understanding the deadlines for your application is very important. By knowing them early on, you will be able better to plan your internal deadlines: to select the dates by which you'd like to get your application completed.

I would recommend that you try to get everything finalized at least two weeks before the submission date, because this would give you enough time to take a break from working on your essays, and allow yourself fresh eyes for the final review. Furthermore, by giving yourself a two-week cushion, you will avoid any unnecessary stress at the very end, when you are rushing to submit everything. After all, human error is possible, and you would much rather be looking for a missing document two weeks before the deadline instead of two hours before it.

To make things more complicated, different universities (mainly for Common App) often offer two to three different types of deadlines. These are **Early Decision** (ED), **Early Action** (EA), and **Regular Decision** (RD).

EARLY DECISION

As the name suggests, this application allows you to apply earlier than the regular admissions pool, giving you a headstart in your application. What is special about this application method is that this is a binding application: if you are accepted, you are obligated to accept the offer. Due to these two factors, universities are more likely to accept students who ED to their university, as it immediately demonstrates your interest in the school, and they are able to rest assured that they would be able to fill a spot in the next year.

EARLY ACTION (EA)

Similar to ED, EA allows you to submit your offers earlier than the rest. This would put you in a different pool to the other candidates, who are applying by RD, and would allow you to secure an offer earlier than the others, giving you more confidence and security during your application process. Unlike ED, the offer isn't binding, so if you get into a university via EA, you are not obliged to accept the offer. What is great about both EA and ED is that even if you don't get accepted at this stage, your application will be placed against the RD application and will still be considered!

REGULAR DECISION (RD)

RD is the most common application deadline that you would use. This deadline is often two months later than the EA/ED deadline, and would give you more time to prepare your application. Obviously, when applying by RD the admissions results would also come back to you later.

By keeping track of the different deadlines for the different platforms and universities that you are applying to, you will be able to make sure that you are on top of things, and will be able to prioritize which essays you should focus on first.

DEADLINE TRACKER

Make sure you write all the deadlines into your notebook. By understanding the deadlines, you will have a clear time-frame to work with when preparing your application!

University	EA/ED Deadline	RD Deadline:

REQUIRED MATERIAL

Much like the deadlines, different universities and platforms often require different materials and tests to be submitted alongside your letters of recommendation, grades, and so on. Therefore, it is important that you make sure that you are aware of these other materials or tests that you need.

LIST OF MATERIALS TO SUBMIT

Generic Materials

These are things that everyone has to submit, regardless of what course they are applying to:

1. *Personal Information:* A boring but essential part of the application process, where you have to fill out family information, your educational background, your passport/ citizenship details, and more.

2. *Past grades/Transcript:* Not only does this show your recent academic achievements, but it also allows universities to track how you have developed as a student over time. Most often, this is sent by your school directly to your university, but you should ask your teachers to find out how this would work.

3. *Activities and Honours section:* The activities and honours section gives you the ability to talk about your academic and extracurricular activities, allowing you to present a more holistic picture of yourself, which cannot be found just within your personal essay. Activities and Honours are separate for the Common App, but are found together for the UCs.

4. *Personal Essays:* These are essays that you will have to submit to the platform, which will then distribute them to all the universities that you are applying to. While the number of these depends on the platform you are applying to, the advice and methods for presenting them are similar.

ADDITIONAL MATERIALS

As said previously, these may change from year to year, and depend on the university, but here are a few extra things you might want to pay attention to:

1. *Language test:* if you are applying from a country where English is not the main language, you may want to check whether you need to do an English Proficiency Test to prove that your English is at the level required for university study.
2. *Standardised Testing:* these are the ACT and the SAT. While most universities are going test-optional (some of them even going test-blind), there is still a section in the Common App to fill out your scores; so if you have done an ACT or SAT, and have achieved a respectable score for your dream universities, feel free to submit them.
3. *Additional work:* certain universities may require you to submit additional material to prove your competence in a certain field of study, and understand more about your background. For example, when applying to Williams, I had the opportunity of submitting a piece of written work to demonstrate my academic ability.
4. *Supplemental essays:* Many universities, especially the more competitive ones, will ask you to submit supplemental essays and

questions to ensure that they have more information, to be able to compare students. These vary from 200-word essays to 20-word answers, so make sure that you are prepared to face a variety of different questions.

5. *Interviews:* Apart from these test materials that you may have to send in, you may also be needed to do an interview. This will give you an opportunity to learn more about the individual university, and allow the university to know more about you as a person, and how you interact with others. Since Covid, most of these have been held online; however, there are a few universities that provide the opportunity to meet in person.

WHAT TO DO NEXT?

In this section, I have discussed some of the most basic admin procedures that you should keep in mind when starting your Common App procedure. While this can be boring, it is important that you keep track of everything to prevent unnecessary angst and mistakes towards the end of your application process. By being well-prepared, you will have an inner state of confidence and peace when approaching your applications.

BUILDING HEALTHY RELATIONSHIPS WITH TEACHERS

It is undeniable that having good relationships with your teachers would be beneficial for your academics, and for your university applications. By having a good relationship with them, you would be able to turn to them for extra material and help when you need it, and when you do need to submit your letters of recommendation, they would be likely to give you a more favourable write-up. So how do you do this?

Rather than going out of your way to be a teacher's pet, a positive relationship with your teachers can be built by working hard in class, showing the teachers that you care about doing well in their subjects, asking questions when you are not sure about something, and making sure that you check up on problems that arise in your homework. What you need to remember is that teachers don't expect you to like their subjects—or themselves. They are mature adults who recognize that no-one needs to like everyone in order to maintain a good working relationship. Focus on paying attention in class! Stop gaming or watching YouTube at the back, and focus on doing your best in your exams and your homework!

Now you might be thinking, "What should I do if I have been irritating my teachers throughout High School?" My message to you is "Don't worry: it isn't too late!"

The first thing I would say is that you shouldn't try to salvage your relationship just for the letters of recommendation. To fake an apology would go against the core message that I am telling you to implement. I am a strong believer in the basic human decency that, if you have not treated others with respect, you should take responsibility and make amends for your mistakes.

The first thing you should do is apologize to your teachers. Yes: you may feel you have been mistreated by your teacher and had every right to be disrespectful. However, that doesn't change the fact that you decided to respond in a less than ideal way. There have been a few times during my High School days where I have had slight disagreements and arguments with my teachers. While I often sent an email on the same day, apologizing for the disrespect shown during class, I rarely changed my stance. Therefore, it is unnecessary to change your stance in order to make an apology.

The second thing is to implement visible change in your routines. If you have been slacking off on homework, make sure you are prompt with your next submissions. If you have been gaming in class or turning up late, make sure you pay attention, and are prompt. You may think that these actions would not get noticed; but trust me, these will make a difference, and will show the teacher that you do care about the course. In the longer term, this would increase the chances of their being willing to write a good letter of recommendation for you.

Now you may be thinking "What if I hate the subject I am doing? You told me to be true to myself, and if that's the case, I should just not do anything!" That could not be further from the truth! Let me tell you a fact about myself. I never liked math: I disliked math so much that I told my math teacher after my GCSEs that he would never see me in a Math classroom again. (I had nothing against the teacher, we had a good, healthy relationship and he was a great guy.) However, I still ended up studying math for the last two years of High School. I have to admit that for a while it was a bit embarrassing, given my bold statements just a few months before. Nevertheless, I gave it my all, to do well in the subject. Why did I do that? Because I take pride in who I am.

> *"A Verse I Keep Present in My Mind*
> *And whatever you do, do it heartily,*
> *as to the Lord and not unto men."*
> **Colossians 3:23 NKJV**

While I may not love doing math, I aim to be someone who is committed, dedicated, and reliable. Even if I don't like doing something, when called to do it, I would make sure that I am giving my all to get it done. In the same way, if you don't like a subject, that's fine! Just make sure you are giving it your best, because that is who you are, and what someone with integrity would be doing.

Now that we have talked about why it is important to build healthy relationships with teachers, and how you can mend mistakes of the past, I would like to advise you to implement these aspects in your life immediately. When I first recognized this reality, not only did my grades increase, but I started enjoying school more. I was driven, I had goals, I was trying to better myself as a student and as a person; and ultimately it led to holistic change and self-improvement.

Now how would this apply to your letters of recommendation?

By having good working relationships with teachers, you would be more confident when asking your teachers to write you a letter of recommendation. Not only would it avoid the awkward undertone of "We both know I've been a sub-par student, but please write something good for me?" It would also mean that the teacher would go above and beyond to write a good letter for you. After all, the best teachers are often asked to write many letters of recommendation. It would be beneficial if you have a good relationship with them, giving them more reason to spend time on your letter rather than the letter of a student who continuously disrespected them over the years.

When it comes to the admin side of the letters of recommendation, each university often has different systems and expectations for the submission process. Some may want one letter, some may want three, some may have requirements for the subject taught by the teachers who write your letters.

After figuring out what the universities are looking for, you would want to choose the appropriate teachers to write your letter of recommendation. This does not need to be a teacher whom you like the most. In fact, sometimes the teachers you get along with best might not be the best teachers to write your letter. Instead, you should find someone with the experience of writing letters of recommendation, and someone who knows who you are.

Once you have found your teachers, I would highly recommend that you ask them as early as possible. This would give them plenty of time to write and edit your letter. Teachers can be very busy, and the last thing you want is for them to rush through your letter.

With all this information in mind, I believe that you will be placed in a very good position to do well in High School and acquire good letters of recommendation—and good grades. Remember, building healthy relationships with your teachers should not just be for your university applications: it would help you make the most of your time in High School.

WHAT ARE ADMISSION OFFICERS LOOKING FOR?

When people ask me for tips about getting into universities, one of the first things I like to do is challenge them with a question: "What do you think the admissions team is looking for and what have you done which would make you the optimal candidate?" While some of them would be able to give an answer, many people would simply waffle, and recognize that they haven't put much thought into the question.

If you are learning a new sport (let's take football for example), the first thing you do is learn what the game's objective is, which is to score more goals than you concede. The same should be true with university admissions! If you don't know what the Admission Officers are looking for, how can you expect to thrive and beat your competition to those precious spots at your dream university?

The best way to understand what the Admissions Officers are looking for is by comparing the US system to the UK system. If you were to look at the UK system, you would immediately see that it only allows for the submission of one personal statement alongside your grades and referral letters. There are no supplemental essays and no activity list that you have to submit on the side. On the other hand, US application platforms not only allow you to submit multiple essays: they also allow you to list anything from 10-20 activities.

This tells us is two things.

Firstly, it shows that US universities are not only looking at how good a student you are for a particular course, but also how you can fit into a certain university, and their vision. If they only cared about your academic ability and passion for the subject, the application process would be similar to the UK's, where you only needed to write a single essay on your academic interests to all the universities. However, the existence of supplemental essays demonstrates that universities want to learn more about you, and get a deeper understanding about you as a person. While many of these supplemental essays may be phrased in a similar way (for example, they mostly include a "why [insert University name]?" question), they are phrased in that way to figure out whether you actually did your research before applying to that university. So make sure you don't fall into the trap of copy and pasting your essays and pay attention to the exact details that the university are asking for.

Secondly, it demonstrates the need for a holistic application. Unlike the UK system, where you need to write about your academic achievements and pursuits, the US universities look for extracurricular strengths as well. For example, while my portfolio is mainly academic, there were occasional parts of my applications where my essays were focused mainly on my charity work, or my football, rarely touching on my academics. Therefore, you should be aware that you do need to learn how to present your portfolio in a way to best represent both your academic and extracurricular strengths.

> *Lessons from a Harvard Student*
> *In a recent interview I shared with a friend at Harvard, his main advice for getting into top US universities comes from "doing a particular thing very very well and doing everything else pretty well". You don't need to be a mathematical genius, a concert pianist, successful entrepreneur and more, but what you do need to do is to show that you are capable in multiple aspects of the human endeavour and also have a speciality to top it off.*

Now this is not to say that you should start participating in activities just for the sake of doing them to fill up the extracurricular quota. As I have said before, many activities that you have already been doing can be very helpful for your university applications. You will be surprised to see how even the most 'academic' profile can be presented with an extracurricular section to demonstrate holistic strength. To demonstrate, both of my friends who have recently got into Harvard applied with mainly academic focused applications. By leading multiple academic societies in school, he was able to teach younger students math. Likewise, as a prefect, he was a role-model for the wider community. As you can see, not everything needs to be 'charity' or 'community service' in the most obvious way to help you demonstrate a "holistic approach".

Therefore, don't be afraid if your application comes off as "too academic". Instead, what would be more productive would be to make sure that you find a way to fit your set of activities into satisfying the other requirements that university Admission Officers are looking for.

By understanding what it is that the Admission Officers are looking for, you will be able to learn how better to prepare for, and structure, your application. While we are going to talk about preparing for your application in more depth later, I do believe that the entire process of choosing and applying to universities should be done with the criteria of the Admission Officers in mind.

DETERMINING WHICH UNIVERSITIES YOU SUBMIT TO

When it comes to your applications, there are very few things which can be as confusing and irritating as how to choose which universities you should apply to, and how you should structure these applications. As a result, I will provide you with two helpful stages to ease you through this process. First, how to rate universities; and secondly, how to categorize your choices into 'safeties', 'matches', and 'reaches'.

RATING UNIVERSITIES

While you can go to a university-ranking website to see which universities are considered the best, you need to recognize that they may be judging these universities on multiple different metrics which may or may not apply to you! Therefore, it is important to go beyond these metrics, and do your research to judge which the best university is for you, coming to your own conclusions.

This is where you will be spending the next four years of your life, and your choice will influence what you get out of your university experience. Therefore I have formulated a set of criteria that you may use to judge the universities that you are interested in.

Of course, this is subjective. Feel free to add or change any of these criteria to suit your needs. However, I do believe that using the following criteria would be a good place to start when thinking about which university is best for you. They may give you some inspiration about the things that you are looking for, specifically to help you decide on your universities.

CRITERION 1: UNIVERSITY REPUTATION

For better or for worse, we live in a world where reputation, clout, and branding are seen as very important. In some ways, one's university is similar to one's outfit. Just as a good outfit might get you attention in the club, the name of your university can help you meet new people and build a stronger network.

Imagine if you were an interviewer for a prestigious internship. You are faced with two identical candidates: one of the candidates is a Harvard alumnus, and the other is from a lesser-known school. Before you even start the interview, it is clear that the one who is a Harvard alumnus would have an advantage before the interview even begins. The similar reasoning can be applied to most other interactions in life. A university with a good reputation can significantly help you get started in your career, by building instant credibility and respect.

Of course, as time goes by and you develop work experience, the initial clout you earn would become less important as people start understanding how you are as a person. However, it would be incorrect to underestimate the usefulness of having a good university diploma to 'back you up'.

> *Story from Josh*
> *Sometimes when I am introducing myself, I feel embarrassed for saying I am studying at Oxford as a lot of the time I get the comment "You must be really smart!" Such a reaction from people who don't know me at all is a good example of how the affiliation to a certain university can increase someone's credibility.*

CRITERION 2: COURSE/DEPARTMENT REPUTATION

While this is normally related to the overall reputation of the university, one should also recognize that different departments in a university have different rankings and reputations. These rankings are based on the number of publications, teaching staff, and other key factors, making it a good indication as to the quality of education you may receive from the department.

In fact, by going to a university with a high department reputation, you would be able to get a head-start in your career, as you would most likely be working with more experienced professors, able to direct you in the right direction, and probably able to help you build your connections.

That said, since US universities are mainly focused on ensuring that students have a holistic education, expect yourself to be working with multiple faculties during your time at the university.

CRITERION 3: FACILITIES

As someone who participates in a wide range of extracurricular activities, I understand how much certain sports or hobbies can mean to you. Therefore, I would highly recommend that you check out the facilities on offer, both by the university and in the nearby city. If you are passionate about a certain extracurricular activity, you might feel disappointed that the facilities are insufficient to support your needs; and in the worst-case scenario, you might need to drop that hobby owing to the lack of facilities. So you should check this out when ranking your universities.

Remember, the facilities don't need to be offered specifically by the university. At Oxford, I use the gym at the local shopping centre instead of the one at the university. You just want to make sure that whatever you want to continue with or try out during your time at university would be made possible by what is on offer in the local town.

CRITERION 4: LOCATION

Related to the facilities is the location of the university. This can be how easy it is to get to the university from home (both as a local or international student); how close it is to the local supermarket or other places you need to access; or whether you feel safe at the university. While the first two may seem like minor inconveniences, you will be living at the university for four years, so you definitely should not overlook these! When I was first talking to my parents about the location of the university, I always told them that it didn't really matter where it was. I felt I was young, and could travel anywhere and it wouldn't change anything.

However, now that I have arrived at university, given the number of times that I travel into London from Oxford, and the frequency that I utilize different facilities in town, I have since realised that the location actually plays a major role in the decision process, and is definitely something that you should bear in mind.

Story from Josh
When I was visiting universities in the US, there were a few universities which I really loved, but which, owing to the location, I decided against applying to. One such university was Johns Hopkins. While I really loved the campus and the lifestyle, I did not enjoy the vibes of Baltimore (where it was located), and on the journey in and out of the campus, the neighbourhood with its broken windows made me feel rather unsafe.

That said, I know people who have studied at, or are applying to, Johns Hopkins, who do not worry, and who enjoy studying there. So make sure you check it out yourself, and if you cannot do so in person, read about it online. Each person has different requirements and tolerances, so make sure you don't just follow what other people say about the university.

CRITERION 5: TEACHING STYLE

Each university provides a different curriculum and teaching style. While most of them would recommend that you take different courses in different disciplines, some enforce this more strictly than others. For example, you can compare

Brown's Open Curriculum to Columbia's Core Curriculum. At Brown, you are way freer to choose the courses that you are interested in, whereas Columbia has certain requirements that you need to fulfil for courses. Likewise, you might be interested in universities which focus on more 1-1 interactions between students and teachers or you may prefer a more lecture like format.

As you can see, each university has their own approach to academics and teaching which may or may not fit what you are looking for. Therefore, make sure you do some research to make sure that the university in interest suits your needs.

CRITERION 6: SOCIAL SCENE AND CULTURE

Another thing you should pay attention to is what the culture is like at the university. Does the university have a very strong drinking and clubbing culture? Is it more academic? Are there social activities on offer that can suit your needs?

While most universities will have facilities and spaces for everyone, it is important to recognize that you will want to be in a place where you feel comfortable and at home.

As a result, make sure that you go check out the culture and social scene at the universities. Not only on their webpages: you can also check forums, or ask people you know who are studying at that university to learn more about it. Depending on your lifestyle, this could be a dealbreaker, and might help you narrow down your choices.

CRITERION 7: THE PEOPLE

To me, this might be one of the most important things when it comes to choosing the university you will be going to. No matter how important academics or extracurriculars may be to you, university is also about meeting new people, improving social skills, and making life-long friends. These people will influence you, and you will influence them. They will help you through tough times, giving you strength when you are weak. However, in a similar vein, if you aren't surrounded by people you think you will fit in among, then they could just as easily have a negative impact on you. You could feel left out, hurt, isolated. Therefore, it is very important to make sure that you try your best to understand what type of people you will most likely come across at the university.

Note from Josh
This doesn't apply only to the student body. If there are any professors who you want to work with, or feel inspired by, you can check out whether they are working or carrying out research at a university you are considering. This could help you make up your mind, and also help you later on with the "Why [insert university name]?" essay.

CRITERIA CHECKLIST

I have created a table which would help you fill out your thoughts on how different universities fulfil your criteria. Of course, each university would naturally be better in some areas and worse in others: I highly doubt that there is a single university which would be a 10/10 in each category. This is why it is important for you to figure out which criteria are more important to you and which ones are perhaps less important for your aspirations.

Criteria	Rate (/10)	Notes
University Reputation		
Department Reputation		
Facilities		
Location		
Teaching style		
Social Scene/ Culture		
The People		
Other (_____)		
Total:		

STRUCTURING YOUR CHOICES

Now I will discuss how you can split your applications into 'safeties', 'matches', and 'reaches'; and also, how many universities you should apply to. Since this is highly subjective, I will aim to provide a general framework which you can apply to your individual situation.

However, before we start, you are probably thinking "Hold on, what on earth are safeties, matches, and reaches?" Well, the answer is quite simple. These are terms used to describe how likely an individual student is to getting into a particular university.

DEFINITIONS

Safety: A university which you would most likely get into.
Match: A university at which your current attainment makes you competitive with the average student at the university (a match).
Reach: A university which is at the upper limits of your potential. More unlikely to get into.

With these definitions in mind, you might still be curious about how you should know whether a university is a safety, a match, or a reach. Unlike in the UK, where you can have a more objective measurement by comparing your grades to the entrance requirements of each university, with US universities it is more difficult.

For starters, judging a holistic student is way less objective than judging a good academic student. If someone has good-enough grades, and can present and articulate their arguments well, you have a clear idea that they are good academics. However, what metrics can you use to judge a good 'holistic' student? What makes a student who does a lot of charity work better than one who is an excellent football player? These problems immediately arise when judging which universities could be considered safeties or not.

Another reason is the common practice called 'yield protection'. This is something universities do to protect a statistic called 'yield'—the number of students who accept their offers, compared with the number of offers that they make. Good examples of these would be people who get accepted by top universities but are rejected by 'less reputable' ones. By throwing in the factor that universities might reject students for being 'too good', can anything be truly regarded as a 'safety'? Perhaps not.

With these two factors in mind, I would like to advise caution, and suggest that unless you live in the US and would not consider studying abroad, you could consider applying to the UK as well. In fact, by submitting just one essay, you have the ability to apply to five universities (making it a very time- and money-efficient decision, especially for safeties). However, if you wouldn't apply to UCAS, one thing you can do is to check the acceptance percentage and the 'yield' of a university. If you believe you are performing way above the level of an average student applying to the university, and the university has high acceptance and low yield, it is more likely that it can be considered a safety. Likewise, if you are performing at the level of the average student at the university, you can consider the university a match. And, of course, if you believe the average student at the university may be better than you, you can consider that university as a reach.

That being said, there are some exceptions. For example, even if you believe you are working at the level of an Ivy League student (and you may be correct), the mere name and inherent competitiveness of the university would make the university a reach, and should not be considered a match for any standard of applicant.

Therefore, in order to learn more about what universities may be considered a safety, match, or a reach, I would highly recommend that you talk to someone in the year above, or to a trusted consultant, and ask them for their overall impression of the acceptance rates of different universities. By understanding these acceptance rates, you will also have a better idea about how you can categorize the universities you are looking at, and how they would fit into the structure for you!

HOW MANY UNIVERSITIES TO APPLY TO

Assuming that you have finally categorised the universities into safeties, matches, and reaches, how many universities you should apply to? This is largely dependent on how efficient you are, and how much time you have left. Personally, I applied to 9 universities with the Common App. As someone who writes quickly, this wasn't a problem for me: as I said, I completed all my essays by the end of December.

However, you will understand yourself best. If you know you write slowly, and each of your universities requires multiple essays, then perhaps you should apply to fewer in order to give yourself enough time to complete all your essays before the deadline. Quality is more important than quantity.

This is also where applying to the University of California has its benefits. Under this system, instead of having to write separate supplemental essays for the individual universities you apply to, you need to write only four personal insight essays, then submit them to whichever UC universities you choose. Of course, you may not be too tempted by studying in California. However, I believe it is another way, apart from applying to the UK, to have a time-efficient safety without needing to put too much extra work into your application: your entire UC application would be the equivalent of applying to 1 Common App university.

That said, regardless of how many universities you are applying to, I believe that there are a few frameworks which will help you distribute your university applications:

1. **Very Ambitious: 20% safety 20% matches 60% reaches**
2. **Ambitious: 20% safety 30% matches 50% reaches**
3. **Moderate: 30% safety 30% matches 40% reaches**
4. **Conservative: 30% safety 40% matches 30% reaches**
5. **Very Conservative: 40% safety 40% matches 20% reaches**

Of course, this is a personal decision. I am not going to recommend one over the other, as each has its own rationale. However, it is also important to recognize that, if you are a naturally ambitious person, and if you applied to too many safeties, you might feel that you have sold yourself short; likewise if you are a bit more conservative, you may prefer to play it safe, as you may feel uncomfortable with the amount of risk you might be taking with only one safety and one match.

That said, there is never any harm in being ambitious. The unpredictable nature of holistic admissions goes both ways! Even if you never thought it was possible to get into your dream university, you never know: so make sure you give it a shot!

> *Reminder from Josh*
> *Remember, everyone has his or her own metric and standards. It is always very easy to be caught up with what other people are applying to, and to feel that you are doing something wrong. Don't worry! Everyone has their own circumstance, everyone has their own story and strategy. I have many friends who were achieving the same grades at school as me: they applied to similar universities, and got far fewer offers. So don't get drawn in or influenced by what other people do. Do what is right for you!*

With these two methods in mind, I believe you will be guided in choosing which universities you should apply to. Not only would you be able to understand more about the individual universities and how they suit your preferences, but you would also be able to split your applications into safeties, matches, and reaches. This would ensure that you have a good chance of getting into your dream universities; but you would also not be too exposed, and end up with no university to go to!

THE ONE-APPLICATION-DREAM-OFFERS METHOD

The **One-Application-Dream-Offers Method**, like the **One-Essay-Five-Offers Method** (for UK applications)—is something that I have developed, based on my experience, and by analysing, with my friends, how we got into the top US universities like Harvard, Columbia, the University of Chicago, UPenn, UC Berkeley, and more. By using this system, we were not only able to get some phenomenal offers, but we were also able to do it by being completely genuine—being true to who we are.

If you are asking why I didn't start off the book by teaching you this method, it is because this wouldn't have worked if you hadn't gotten the fundamentals right. In fact, everything I've told you so far has been building the foundation on which you may build to apply this method to your applications. The reality is that there are two ways to approach university admissions.

- Firstly, you try to think about what some of the things are that are "good for university admissions," then throw away everything else that doesn't fall into that basket.
- Secondly, you develop yourself into a good person who is talented and extraordinarily capable in many different areas

While the first might seem like an easy way to get into your dream university, from my analysis, such a mindset does not seem to be productive for success. However, if you follow what I have been telling you in this book, you will realize that what I've been doing all along is trying to develop you into the second type of applicant. You are someone who recognises the importance of university admissions, but also has the maturity to see beyond this, into the bigger picture which is your life and future.

It is for this reason that I have structured the book in the way that I have done! By getting your relationships with teachers in order, by getting your academics in order, by getting your life in order, you will have already built up a portfolio that includes everything you need for submitting a good application.

I will spend this chapter discussing how you can use the foundation that you already have developed, to formulate a convincing application that will get you into your dream universities.

Since there are three different types of material you need to consider when applying to your university, I have split this chapter into three sections.

- Firstly, how to prepare your application.
- Secondly, how to write your essays, your activities and honours section, and your supplemental essays.
- And finally, how to edit and submit them.

By going through these three vital stages, you will have a better understanding as to how you can submit the best application, and put yourself in the best position to get into your dream university.

Of course, there will be differences between the UC system, the Common App system, Questbridge, and more. However, the techniques and stages used to write the individual essays are the same, and can be generally applied across the platforms. If you would like more a more specific analysis of the Common App and the UCs, the two most common platforms, you could check out the courses we have made at Logos Education. Those would walk you through the exact process that each platform requires.

1. PREPARING YOUR APPLICATION

In order to submit a competitive application, it is important to make sure that your preparation is perfect. This means that instead of picking up the pen immediately and trying to write something down, you should take a step back and gather your thoughts, making sure that your application is well-formulated.

Remember when I talked about how a chess player thinks through moves in advance, and does everything deliberately?

You need to ensure that everything you do from now on is done with purpose and direction.

Unlike the UK system where you only need to think about how you present yourself in one essay, with the US system you need to remember that your application is split over your core essays, supplemental essays, and activity sections.

If you find this confusing, don't worry. I have put together a set of tips that you can use to prepare your application. These tips are based on the information already discussed in this book, and will give you a competitive edge over your fellow applicants, who are unaware of this advice. As long as you follow this information, I am certain that you will feel more confident in your application.

TIP 1:
DO A LIFE AUDIT

The first thing that I want you to do before everything else is to make a mind-map of what you have done, and what you are currently doing. Previously, I told you to take inventory of what you were currently doing. Feel free now to go over that mind-map and extend it to what you have done in previous years.

Now, it might be tempting to just write down a few highlights for each year, but I would really suggest that you take a deep look at yourself. Reflect on the highs and lows of each year, allow yourself to reminisce about the past, what you learned from certain activities, certain mistakes you made, and also things that you have done better.

Whenever you come across a significant activity, write it down—and note down its impact! See how those skills have been applied and have developed over the years, and how they have made you into the person you are today. Perhaps you regretted being too harsh with your words during an argument in Freshman year, making enemy of a dear friend—which however led to growth in self-control and wisdom? Perhaps you later became the football-team captain, or a prefect; and that resulting self-awareness helped you navigate difficult and high-pressure situations? These things, though they might seem irrelevant at first, are things which you should be paying attention to.

Unlike in the UK, where these individual extracurricular stories may be less important to the personal statement, given the holistic outlook of US admissions, and how essay questions are framed, these stories might come in handy to demonstrate growth and self-understanding.

Furthermore, doing a life audit will also allow you to remember activities that you might have forgotten, but which might be helpful in supporting the claims you make in your application. By having your memory refreshed, you will find it easier to write about (and support) the claims that you will be making in your application.

After you finish making this mind-map, I would like you to rank the activities in order of importance; and then proceed to colour-code the activities into different categories, like academic, charity, sport, or community. Of course, these will overlap. However, having an idea of the individual activities that you have participated in will give you a better understanding of what you can put into your different application sections. Your more important activities and stories can be placed in your core essays; the secondary activities can be put into your activities and honours list; and the other supporting information can be placed into your supplemental essays.

Of course, depending on the prompts you are working with, the applicability of the activities would change. However, a general rule of thumb is that your activities should be distributed throughout the application, and should not be repeated more than twice. Of course, if you want to elaborate on something on your activities list, by all means repeat it. However, if you repeat the same activity four or five times, the Admission Officer would most likely think that you are running out of examples and activities, suggesting that you do not have enough experience to support your claims.

TIP 2:
WRITE DOWN 5 REASONS WHY YOU WANT TO STUDY AT THE UNIVERSITY, AND WHY YOU WOULD FIT IN THERE

Let us recall what the admission officers are looking for. They are looking for applicants who want to study at their university and are good matches for the college culture that they are trying to build.

With this in mind, it is important that you do your research to figure out why you want to study at the university, and also how you would fit into the identity and vision of the university.

You might think that this is extremely time-consuming: the reality is that it is! However, by doing in-depth research, you will be able to understand whether you really want to study at this university, or whether you had misconceptions about it in the first place. By figuring out whether you really want to apply to that university and eliminating certain universities from your list, you could save valuable time and effort.

Now that you have carried out your research, it is important that you write down 5 reasons why you want to study at the university, and 5 ways in which you fit into the university's vision. These are things that you want to demonstrate in your supplemental essays, and if there is significant overlap across the universities, you could work these ideas into your core essays and activity lists as well.

> *Story from Josh*
> *In our research about universities, Warren and I decided that the best way to understand more about each university was to read through all the individual pages, including their diversity, inclusivity policies, and more. While this might seem extreme, the reality is that a lot can be learnt from how they phrase and present different societal issues, and how they aim to solve or avoid them. By doing so, you would understand more about the culture, and how you could fit into the vision that they are trying to build.*

TIP 3: DON'T TALK TO YOUR PEERS

Firstly, this will give you a false sense of security. When I started writing my application in the first few weeks of Senior Year, I was met with shock, and by people telling me that I was starting way too early. The reason why this can be negative is that if you hear consistently that you have a lot of time left, you might begin to feel that since you are starting way ahead of everyone else, you can take it half-heartedly until everyone else starts working.

While it is true that I am telling you to get started before everyone else, the purpose of this is precisely to give you more than enough time to get your applications in order.

Therefore, it wouldn't be beneficial to talk to too many of your peers about your university application process.

> **Note from Josh**
> *Three hours before the application deadline, a good friend of mine called me and asked me to proofread his application essays. Let's just say that this was one of my most hectic experiences. I was busy deconstructing, providing suggestions, and analysing his essays while he was trying his best to implement the suggestions within the short time-frame. So— make sure you don't follow what everyone else is doing, and that you stick to your own schedule.*

Secondly, your peers may not know what they are talking about! We all know those people who like to act as though they know everything, when in reality they are just unwilling to say, "I actually have no clue what is going on". Therefore, instead of trying to get more advice, make sure that instead you are targeting quality advice.

There would definitely be some peers who do know what they are doing, and if you know who those are, then by all means talk to them. But the majority of your peers are most likely to be in the same boat as you are when it comes to admissions advice. Hence, instead of trying to separate the wheat from the chaff with regard to what they are saying, save your time by just getting started, and working on preparing your personal statement.

TIP 4:
TALK TO PEOPLE WHO KNOW WHAT THEY ARE DOING

Tied to the advice provided in Tip 3, I would suggest that you talk to the five people whom you think are most knowledgeable about university admissions. This may be your university consultant officer, an older student who has gotten into one of your dream universities, an experienced tutor, or someone else whom you trust.

By talking to them and asking them for their best tips and tricks for getting into the top universities, you would be able to learn what you should do in your application. Furthermore, don't only ask them questions about what you should do, but also ask them what you shouldn't do. By learning from their mistakes and what they could have done better, you would be able to act on what they did well, and be more efficient by avoiding their mistakes.

Remember, the most successful students are those who are able to analyse and learn from their mistakes. As a result, make sure that you are surrounding yourself with successful people, so that you will be able to avoid the major pitfalls that they fell into.

That said, I would recommend you not to talk to too many people. After all, each person would have their own conception of what is considered to be a good application. By talking to too many people, you may receive rather conflicting advice, and end up even more confused about what you should do.

TIP 5:
READ SUCCESSFUL ESSAYS

There is nothing which would help you more than getting your hands on a set of successful applications and analysing them. While it is preferable that these are for the universities that you are applying to, just learning how people have approached different prompts can be really helpful.

Go to your school's inhouse consultant, or the teacher they have in charge of university admissions. You can ask them if they have any example essays on hand. If they don't have any, you can check out the application course at Logos Education (www.logos-education.com) to look at the Common App and Supplemental Essays which got me into Columbia, Boston College, Notre Dame, and more. Furthermore, you can reach out to successful friends in the year above, and see if they would share their essays with you.

By reading their essays, you would be able to get a feel of the different structures and methods that they used to develop their ideas and arguments. By analysing them and noticing common trends, you would be able to learn what the Admission Officers are looking for, and you would be able to adapt their ideas for your essay.

I am not asking you to go copy their work, nor am I telling you to do everything that they are doing in their essays. After all, it is important that you maintain your voice and identity throughout your application. But I would invite you to really try to consider the essays from the perspective of the Admission

Officer and think "Why did this essay get in over another one?" "What makes this essay special?"

By doing so, I believe you would gain a better understanding and perspective when it comes to writing your own application, and would be shown you how to develop your ideas in a convincing manner, to give yourself the competitive edge.

By following these five tips, you would be in a very good place to start your application process. Not only would you have a better understanding of your portfolio, and how different activities may fit into different parts of your application, but you would also have a good understanding of what makes a good application—which you can then implement in writing your own essays and activity list.

2. WRITING YOUR APPLICATION

Give yourself a pat on the back for all the hard work you have put into yourself, and by extension into your application, during your High School years. I know the journey will have had its ups and downs. There will have been times when you felt that you had been on a winning streak and had been making one good decision after another; and there will have been other times where you may have felt that you made less than optimal choices.

However, that's life: and if you had the mental fortitude to carry on, and been perspicacious enough to learn from your mistakes, then I am certain that you are one step closer to achieving your full potential! The reality is, as much as we may imagine that Admission Officers are looking for perfect end products, that isn't something which is healthy or helpful. It is more important to learn how you can present your mistakes and flaws in a positive light, in order to demonstrate your development and increasing wisdom.

In this chapter, I will discuss how you can present your application in the best way possible. I will cover how you can write your personal essays, your activity lists, and supplemental essays, to suit the requirements and the criteria of the Admission Officers. Of course, each platform has its own set of materials you'll need to submit. For example, the Common App will ask for a personal essay, an activity list, and supplemental essays, whereas the UCs ask for four personal insight questions and an activity list, without any supplemental essays. However, the tips for how to prepare each section are fairly broadly applicable, and I will cover them together in this book.

3. WRITING YOUR PERSONAL ESSAY

Let me preface everything by stating that there is no 'one formula' for writing an amazing personal essay. With the wide range of essay prompts, individual stories, backgrounds, and experiences, it would be ludicrous for anyone to even suggest that following their one way would be a guarantee of success.

For this reason, when approaching the personal essay (for Common App) or the personal insight questions (for UCs), it is vital that you take a step back and critically analyse where you are at, and then figure out how your portfolio can fit into what the prompts are looking for.

In order to do this, I have made a list of four tips to ensure that you have a good foundation for starting to write your application.

TIP 1:
READ ALL THE PROMPTS

When approaching the personal essay, the first thing you would realize is that there are multiple prompts available for you to choose from. This instantly provides the applicant with multiple questions. Which prompt should you choose? Which prompt is more beneficial for your application? Is there a specific prompt which is objectively better than the rest?

The reality is that the best prompt to choose is the one which would allow you to showcase yourself and present your skill-set in the best way possible. The admission officers recognize that everyone's profile is different, and the variety of prompts are there so that no matter who you are, and no matter what background you have, there should be a prompt which best matches your profile and will allow you to demonstrate your strengths. Furthermore, when you read the prompts closely, while they are phrased differently, they are all trying to accomplish the same thing—to allow the Admission Officer to understand who you are as a person, and how you have developed over the years.

Therefore, when you are reading through the prompts, I would like you to write down your initial thoughts and ideas about each one of them. Perhaps brainstorm a potential answer to several of the prompts, to see whether you have more to say in response to one prompt or the other. By doing so, not only would you discover which prompt is the best for you; you would also begin to see common themes and traits shared by the prompts, helping you to pinpoint what the Admission Officers are looking for.

> *Tip from Josh*
> *Don't jump into writing and preparing for just one prompt. Unless you properly test multiple prompts, you will never know whether there is another prompt which may suit you better!*

After planning for a number of the prompts, then you should start eliminating the ones which really don't fit you; and depending on whether you need to write one (Common App) or four (UC) essays, then cut the prompts down to that number.

If you find it difficult to cut the choices down, perhaps prepare the essay further—maybe even write a simple draft for the ones you have left. This would give you a better understanding of how the prompts bring out different parts of your portfolio, and which ones suit you best.

TIP 2:
THINK ABOUT THE FEATURES THAT YOU WANT TO PRESENT

In the last tip, I suggested how you should brainstorm each prompt to see which one you have most affinity with. After you have chosen the prompt that you have the best connection with, I would like you to spend some time developing those initial drafts and building on the things that they contain. Make sure that what you are planning is directly answering the prompt, and doesn't go off on a tangent.

As much as you may want to do something 'different', or 'show off' your entire repertoire of skills and talents, it is better to answer the question directly. This is especially important for the UC system. Since you are writing four essays, you want to make sure that everything you present, including your activities list and supplemental essays, is like a jigsaw puzzle, each of them combining to form a cohesive image of who you are as a person. Therefore, don't repeat things: be precise with your words and what you are saying.

One tip which I found especially helpful is that you can use a story as a foundation for each of your essays. For example, while my Common App essay was based on my interactions with people while fishing in Central Park, I supported the story with charity-work in Mongolia, my affinity for political discourse, my composure in high-intensity situations, and more. Likewise, if you are presenting your strengths in football, you can then talk about a time where you mentored a younger player in the team when they were going through a tough time; or perhaps how you were always willing to put your body on the line to help your team succeed.

While such a small event might not make its way into the supplemental essay or the activity list, it adds a personal touch to the personal essay, and will allow you to demonstrate how each of your activities can be tied to further themes, like serving the community, and charity-work.

Furthermore, stories are a great way to 'show and not tell'. Each activity that you describe yourself in would tell the officers a lot about your personality. From my going fishing, an Admission Officer would immediately know that I am someone who is patient and loves nature. Being a footballer would suggest that you can work in a team-work with other people to achieve a common goal. Of course, there will always be impatient fishermen and selfish footballers! However, these are still good ways to demonstrate a wider range of skills and traits that you have, without having to describe them directly.

TIP 3:
TELL A GOOD STORY

Developing on the message in the previous tip, the most important thing you want to keep in mind is that your personal essay is a story. Of course, the story will vary depending on the prompt, and sometimes it will be more academic than at other times. But you need to recognize that the Admission Officers are only trying to figure out who you are, and how you have developed over the years, making your application quite literally a story of your life.

If you approach it as you do when telling a story, this will automatically make it way more interesting than if you wrote in a formal, academic tone. Therefore, don't be afraid to let your personality shine through the essay: let loose with your creativity and your ideas.

What this also means is that you should structure it like a story. Unlike an academic paper—where you state everything that you will be arguing in the introduction, then proceed to dissect the premises of the argument in each paragraph—you will want to follow the framework of a story.

Write a hook to draw the reader in. Perhaps start the essay with a problem that you faced, and use the rest of the essay to describe how you overcame it. Perhaps provide multiple problems that you have faced, throughout the essay, each more difficult than the other. By doing so, you would create an engaging application that will make the Admission Officer want to know more about you, and feel that you would make an interesting member of their community.

> *Funny Story from Josh*
> *You would not have guessed it, but a good friend of mine got into John Hopkins with a story about cooking egg fried rice! He used his experience of cooking Asian dishes to demonstrate a wide variety of skills and personality traits which made his application unique and stand out!*

TIP 4: WRITE FIRST, THINK LATER

I have always stressed doing your preparation correctly. However, once you feel confident with your preparation, I highly recommend that you start writing at once, and think less about the minute details of word count, grammar, and overall smoothness.

If you follow the schedule that I have set out, you should have more than enough time to refine and edit your application, to get it to the final product.

As someone who writes around ten thousand words a week on a regular basis, I know from experience that the toughest part about writing is always how to get started and produce the first draft. The editing and refining can come later, and is always easier to do than just getting your ideas down.

Therefore, don't make the mistake of focusing too specifically on the small details and sacrificing the impetus and inspiration you may feel at the start of your writing journey.

Bonus tip: Do not fall into identity politics
While US universities often get the reputation of being 'liberal' and in love with identity politics, you would be ill-advised to base your application purely on the fact that you were born into some minority group.

While there are things like affirmative action which can potentially increase your chances of getting into a university, if your essay is solely focused on how you are a member of the LGBTQ+ community, it is clear that your essay would not be very strong.

This is not to say that you should never raise it! If you do, make sure it ties into an overarching story or theme, and does not feel redundant, or like a mere passing remark. The worst thing you can do is try to focus so hard on one element of your identity such that you fail to present all the other worthy parts of your application.

By following these five tips, I believe that you will have a better understanding of how you can write a phenomenal personal essay. Get writing! Don't worry about small details. The editing will come later. Right now, focus on finishing your first draft so that you can move on to writing your activity and honours list.

4. WRITING YOUR ACTIVITIES AND HONOURS LIST

The reason why I discuss the activities and honours list prior to discussing supplemental essays is that they are going to be sent to every university. By the time you get to your supplemental essays (if you are not applying to the UCs), you will know which activities have already been listed, and which ones can be used to further supplement your application.

Before you start writing, I would like you to return to the activity list that you created during your life audit. After refreshing your mind on which ones you are still to use, I would recommend that you write a description, as per the requirements of the application system, about each activity.

Tip from Josh
Don't worry if you have too many activities. In fact, it is better to write descriptions for many activities, and have some to spare, than it would be to run out. When I first put my list of activities together, I had twenty-plus activities. Instead of narrowing them down immediately, I decided to elaborate on all of these activities before placing them into the activity section.

By describing each activity before committing to which ones you will eliminate, you will realize that some activities are way easier to analyse than others are. For example, travelling yearly to Mongolia to help a charity is way easier to write a description of, compared with being the Head Editor of the school's humanities publication. Therefore, by carrying out this preparation you will soon realize which activities should be kept in the activity sections, which ones can be placed in the honour section, and which ones can be distributed to your supplemental essays—or even retrospectively added to your personal essays.

As to the order of your activities, it is important to rank them in order of importance. While it would be nice if Admission Officers read every single activity that you wrote down, it is important to remember that they are reading thousands and thousands of applications. As a result, it is important that your first three activities hook the Admission Officer in. If they don't, the Officer might end up skimming or skipping the remainder of the list, which will put you at a significant disadvantage. Therefore, your activity list should always start with the most interesting and important activities, inviting the Admission Officers to read on.

However, after your first three activities, I would recommend that you split the rest of the activities into different categories. For example, you shouldn't have all your first five activities academic, with the rest focused on extracurricular activities. Rather, I would recommend that you mix them up so that the Admission Officer has the feeling that you have diverse interests, following different pursuits, and that your activity list isn't the result of copying and pasting two academic and extracurricular lists together.

The last thing you should bear in mind is that you should make sure that you don't state the obvious in the descriptions. The application already gives you very little space to elaborate on the activities. Don't waste any words on describing things which can be clearly deduced from the activity name. For example, if one of the activities is your YouTube channel, you do not need to add "make videos" in the description. The time would be better spent talking about the content that you may be posting.

By following these tips, you should be able to put together a very comprehensive activities and honours list, placing you in a very good position to move on to writing your supplemental essays.

5. WRITING YOUR SUPPLEMENTAL ESSAY

Since there are so many different types of supplemental essays, they cannot all be approached in the same way, and should be treated differently. However, by approaching them with these tips in mind, I believe you will have a clear direction for what you need to do.

> *Note from Josh*
> *If you are only applying to the UCs, then this would not apply to you. Therefore, use this time for improving your UC application; spend more time editing your application.*

TIP 1: RECAP WHAT THE UNIVERSITIES ARE LOOKING FOR

The first thing you need to think about is why universities have supplemental essays. If each university cared about the same metrics and information, they would, like the UK, only ask you to submit one essay, or a generic application, to the Common App. Nevertheless, they allocate additional time and effort to ensure that they read through all the supplemental essays required of applicants.

The only reason for doing this is that they believe that the supplemental essays will give them vital information in judging which students are the right ones for them. Therefore, I would like you to spend some time in recapping what the universities are looking for.

Don't only recap what you wrote down on your list, but go to their website, and talk to any current students you may know. Try to figure out what campus life is like, and what the university's vision is! By doing this, you will be able to fit your response to what the universities are looking for in the best possible way.

This doesn't mean that you should try to change your voice and your intentions to fit into the university's vision. If they are looking for a completely different mould of student, you probably shouldn't apply. However, if you have already done your research about the university, you should realize that there would be more similarities than differences regarding your visions.

TIP 2:
RECAP WHY YOU WANT TO STUDY AT THE UNIVERSITY

Not only would this help you write the very common "Why [insert university's name]?" question; it would also help you get into the right framework to write your essays. While this is something you should have already thought about when choosing universities, by recapping these reasons, and elaborating on them, you would have the upper hand when it comes to submission.

If you are only writing the essays half-heartedly, the essays will come off as unconvincing, and would not be as competitive when compared to someone who really wants to attend the university in question. This is not to say that you must love every single university you are applying to. However, I am sure that each university you are applying to, including your safeties, should have at least a handful of reasons that make it attractive to you. If not, you should probably look to apply to another university. There are so many universities out there, and there would always be a fit for you, even if it isn't as 'competitive' as you might like it to be!

> *Story from Josh*
> *Despite getting phenomenal offers from all the best universities in the world, ranging from Oxford, to Columbia, to St. Andrews, to Notre Dame, when I was making my decision on which university to attend, my second choice, behind Oxford, was a close draw between Columbia and Wheaton Illinois.*

TIP 3: PAY ATTENTION TO THE PROMPT

If you are applying to a lot of universities, you would soon notice that many prompts may start to sound similar, or may seem to be asking for the same information. This is only natural. While they are looking for different things, there is only so much a university can ask or expect from a seventeen-year-old. Therefore, even if the question is worded completely differently, you might have the intuition that you can just copy and paste another supplemental essay, and change a few words. However before you do that, you need to remember that the slightly different formulations are there for a reason.

Apart from the fact that the officers may know each other, and may talk about what they have read, you could end up missing the point, and answering a totally different question if you only rely on copy and paste.

Now this is not to say that copy and paste is off-limits: there will be questions where you can keep the majority of one essay and change certain details to make it relevant to another prompt. Doing so can save precious time and effort. That said, approach it with caution and care, and you need to make sure that you are still answering the prompt in the best way possible.

TIP 4:
APPLY THE WRITING ADVICE FOUND FOR PERSONAL ESSAYS

A lot of the advice about how to write a good personal essay can also be applicable here. To recap, these are:

1. **Write first, think later.**
2. **Write a good story.**
3. **Don't get caught up with 'identity'.**

By following these tips, I believe you would be in a very good place to write a good first draft for your supplemental essays. At this point, don't worry too much about the small details of your first draft. These take time to iron out, and a lot may change over the editing process. Right now, just focus on getting the first draft of your application together. After you do that, you should then focus on editing your application, which we will turn to now.

EDITING YOUR APPLICATION

Now that we have discussed how you can write your application, we will discuss how you can get from that first draft to the submission version. In my opinion, this should be the longest stage in the **One-Application-Dream-Offer Method**. No matter how good your first draft is, there will always be ways in which you can refine it to fit the admission requirements.

In this chapter, I will give you a six-step plan which you can use to make sure that your application is at the right place. Even though essays and activity lists are slightly different, the people to whom you should turn for advice are the same, and I have combined these together.

STEP 1: RE-READ YOUR APPLICATION

The first thing I want you to do is to re-read your application three times. Ask yourself, "Does this sound smooth; are there any problems with the spelling and grammar; am I presenting myself clearly?"

By doing this, you will be able to have your first draft in a better and more accessible form. This would allow for the remaining steps to be focused on the content, instead of on relatively minor issues like spelling and grammar. You can also cut down on unnecessary words like adjectives and adverbs, and start prioritising which activities are more important than others, allowing you gradually to reduce the word-count to fit into the word limit.

One thing which is especially helpful for cutting down words in the activity section is to make sure that you make the most out of each space provided. For example, if you are running out of space in the description, you can move some of it (where possible) to the organization description. For example, instead of naming your Podcast in the description, name it in the organization, and perhaps put the ranking there as well.

Furthermore, if you are not a native English-speaker, it might be helpful to have a native speaker read through the application for you. By doing so, they may be able to point out linguistic nuances which you, as a foreigner, may not be aware of. As someone who can speak Spanish, although I can read it, and carry out conversations with natives, I would always make subtle mistakes. While it is clear what I am trying to say, it may come across as awkward, or slightly off. In the same way, if you are not a native speaker, it could be very helpful to get a native speaker to read it for you, to make sure that your application doesn't include similar pitfalls.

STEP 2:
SHOW IT TO SUCCESSFUL APPLICANTS

I would then recommend you to show your application to successful applicants, preferably a friend in the year above, being your friend, they would be able to tell you whether your essay successfully represents who you are as a person and tell you whether your voice is clear throughout the application. These are things that a teacher or a professional cannot help you with. Your friends know you best, and even if you have the best application "on paper", an authentic, true glimpse into who you is greatly valuable.

> *Story from Josh*
> *Balancing activities and retaining your voice can be quite difficult. For example, when I was editing one of my friend's essays, I found it difficult to suggest content changes without completely changing his voice. After all, this friend is one of those people who had such a distinct way of speaking and writing that I felt it would be a shame if that was hindered in any way. Therefore, if you feel like there is a conflict between the content and your voice, you should take care in making sure that you find a good balance between the two.*

Furthermore, if you talk to your friends at the university that you are applying to, they would be able to give you insider information about what the university is looking for. Having studied at the university, they may be able to give you feedback which others may not know. Therefore, having a good network of friends can definitely help you hugely in your application process.

STEP 3: IMPLEMENT CHANGES, AND RE-READ IT TWICE

After hearing from your friends, I would like you to go back home and ponder on their feedback, and on how you can best implement it into your essay. After doing so, you should then implement the suggestions which you feel enrich the content in your application, then re-read the essay twice.

Unlike with Step 1, I would recommend that you only check for minor errors in the first re-read. Every time the material changes, there is always the opportunity for errors to creep into your application. However, after you've read it once, I would like you to re-read it and check whether you can still clearly see your identity within the essays, and whether the changes have helped to develop your essay.

One thing you should never do is to follow someone's advice so closely that the essay is no longer is *yours*, and that your voice fades out of the essay. It is important to keep both the content and your voice in mind when approaching this stage of editing!

> *Side note*
> *This applies to all of the editing steps. If you are seeking advice, make sure that you remember that the essay is yours, not the person's to whom you are going for advice.*
> ***Don't feel bad about ignoring some things that people tell you to do!***

STEP 4:
SHOW IT TO A CONSULTANT/ADVISOR

I would highly recommend showing your application to a university consultant or advisor. Depending on where you're studying, this might be your school's consultant, or someone you've hired; or you can reach out to my team at Logos Education to get your essay analysed. We offer both 1-1 consultant calls, and essay reviews. By doing this, you will get advice from people who are familiar with the admissions process.

By the time you talk to a consultant, the help they are offering you is less about the actual academics and extracurricular activities: rather, they are there to make sure that everything you have written so far makes sense, and is well put together, to get into your dream universities.

If you have done very well so far, then they probably won't need to do very much. After all, if you have your academics in a good place alongside your extracurriculars, then you should already have a very good application. However, by turning to an expert, you will be able to get that final stamp of approval before you send the application off.

STEP 5: REPEAT STEP 3

STEP 6: SUBMIT

After you have re-read your work and feel confident about what you have provided, then it is time to submit your application to the universities. By following this preparation and reaching out for help whenever needed, I believe your essays will be in a very good place for getting you into your dream universities.

CONCLUSION

We have reached the conclusion of the **One-Application-Dream-Offers Method**. By reading this book, I hope you will have a better understanding of what you will need to do going forward, regardless of where you are in the university admissions process. As seen in this book, regardless of what your time-frame is, if you follow the steps below, and especially those in the previous chapter, there is no excuse for your not to being able to submit an extremely successful application.

To end this book, I would like to do two things. Firstly, to give you a rough plan for what you need to do next; and secondly, if you still have any questions or want any of this content to be discussed in more depth, I will direct you to more material and resources that have been put together.

WHAT TO DO NEXT?

Before I talk about what you can do next, let me summarize what we have covered in this book.

1. The first thing you need to do is get your life in order and make sure that your actions are well-thought-out and deliberate.
2. Make sure you work hard in building your personal identity and story, in the process making sure that you try your best in everything you do.
3. Make sure to complete the admin stuff on the Common App first.
4. Make sure your relationships with your teachers are in the right place.
5. Make sure to pay attention to what the Admission Officers are looking for.
6. Spend quality-time preparing your application.
7. Write first, think later.
8. Take time in editing your application, and reach out for professional and expert advice if you need help.

The next thing you need to do is to go and follow these steps, and apply them to your application.

Remember, depending on where you are, this may be a one-month, one-year, or even a five-year process. So make sure you recognize your time-frame, and plan your next actions accordingly. Like the chess player, don't leave anything to chance: make sure you are deliberate and purposeful in everything you do.

Now don't expect to see instant success. Some of the most painstaking and important moments of the process of self-improvement (which is the fundamental message of this book) comes when everything seems to be going against you. I've been there myself—trust me, it can hurt at times. However, keep going, keep working on self-improvement and your personal identity! Don't give up!

I promise you this! If your heart is in the right place, you will be at peace, and happy with where you are during your university years!

That is the most important thing!

So get started! Don't procrastinate: embark on this journey towards success! Embark on this journey towards your dream university.

FURTHER HELP AND RESOURCES

You might feel that you still don't know exactly what you need to do. Don't worry, this process can be overwhelming. There is only so much I could fit into this book without it's becoming as long as the Oxford English Dictionary. Furthermore, if you are considering applying in the UK as well as in the US, you might have absolutely no idea of what to do for that!

In order to help you further, I have put together a list of different services and materials that I have created to cover every aspect of university admissions, both for the UK and the US. I've also added a few links to direct you to web-pages which I regularly update with university news and advice, so that you can have access to content on university admissions.

US ADMISSIONS TOOLS

1. *Common App Application Course:* **This online course covers and expands upon the content provided in this book, illustrating the concepts with visuals and graphics to make the information easier to digest. It analyses the individual ideas in more depth, and provides further tips and tricks. So if you want to learn more about the Common App, make sure you check it out here: https://www.logos-education.com/common-app-course**

2. *UCs Admissions Course:* **Another application system in America, which you may be interested**

in applying to, is the UCs. While it is similar to the Common App system, in the sense that there are essays and activities lists that you have to fill out, there are notable differences as well. If you are interested in applying to the UCs, but are not sure how to get started, make sure you go check out the UC admissions course on Logos Education. This can be found here: https://www.logos-education.com/uc-admissions-course

3. *Interview Course:* While most universities do not require interviews, some of the top universities do offer an interview to allow the university to learn more about you, and for you to ask an alumnus more about the university. If you want to learn how to ace an interview, make sure you check out this course, where I talk about the fundamentals of mastering any interview, so that you can enter it with confidence and composure. Check it out here: https://www.logos-education.com/interview-course

4. *1-1 Consulting Session:* As I have said throughout this book, the information on these courses and in the book is all generic, and is written to be applicable to every applicant. If you would like to discuss your individual portfolio and application, you can book a 1-1 consulting call with me at Logos Education. This can be to plan what you need to do next, answer any questions, work through an essay, or anything related to university admissions: https://www.logos-education.com/consulting

5. *Essay Reviews:* If you would like to get your essays reviewed by a member of our team, then make sure you check out the different plans we offer here: https://www.logos-education.com/essayreviews

UK ADMISSION COURSES

If you are interested in applying in the UK as well as in the US, then make sure to check out the following courses and materials to guide you through the UCAS process!

1. *The UCAS Bible:* If you enjoyed this book and found it helpful, you will also enjoy *The UCAS Bible* which follows the structure found in this book to help you get into your dream UK universities. This can be found on our website or on Amazon: https://www.logos-education.com/ucas-bible

2. *UK UCAS Application Course:* This course covers the content provided in *The UCAS Bible*, illustrating the concepts with visuals and graphics to make the information easier to digest. Furthermore, it will analyse the individual ideas in more depth and provide further tips and tricks. So if you want to learn more about the UCAS application, make sure you check it here: https://www.logos-education.com/ucas-admissions-course

3. *Oxbridge Application Course:* **If you are applying to Oxbridge and are not sure what to do about written work, subject tests, the interview, and more things related to Oxbridge applications, this course will cover what these extra materials are, and how you can prepare yourself to get into some of the top universities in the UK. If you want to check this course out, find it here: https://www.logos-education.com/oxbridge-application-course**

MORE TOOLS AND WEBSITES

1. *Logos Education:* **Logos Education aims to provide high-quality and affordable university admissions advice to people from all backgrounds. If you want to learn more about university admissions and do not know where to start, you can check out our website, and see what services best suit your needs! You can find the website here: https://bit.ly/logosedu**

2. *My Personal Website:* **By staying up to date with my personal website, you would not only have access to exclusive information about university admissions and High School advice: you would also stay up to date with all my latest publications and work. You can find my website here: www.josh-yen.com**

ABOUT THE AUTHOR

Joshua Yen is currently a student at the University of Oxford, reading Philosophy and Theology. While a rigorous academic, having published the book *Christianity for All*, and several articles on themes relating to philosophy, theology, and literature, he also has a vision to help students and the youth of today reach their full potential, whether in academics or beyond. In order to reach this goal, he also spends the majority of his free time running three YouTube channels (which have amassed a following of over 4,000 subscribers) and his recent business venture, Logos Education, providing university application advice to people all over the world.

In Joshua's eyes, there are few things more vital in High School than the question of university! Should I go to university? What should I study? How do I get into the top universities? This book and Logos Education are prime examples of how he intends to use his extensive knowledge, having gotten into the best universities around the world like Oxford, Columbia, UCL, St Andrews, and more, to help others who are wrestling with these existential questions to achieve their full potential in High School and beyond.

On the side, when he is not working on his undergraduate degree or his business pursuits, he spends his time fishing, playing football, and travelling. Having set foot in almost every continent on earth (*sans* South America), Joshua has had the experience of meeting many wonderful people, and interacting with different cultures—using this experience to further his understanding of the world, and to enrich the educational content he provides on his platforms.

Joshua's motto in life is simple. "To serve God, to serve the family, and to serve the community!"

If you would like to get in touch with Joshua for podcast appearances, video shows, speaking, and other interactions, feel free to reach out at: admin@logos-education.com

Made in the USA
Monee, IL
09 September 2023